Forty Voices Strong
An Anthology of Contemporary Scottish Poetry

Forty Voices Strong
An Anthology of Contemporary Scottish Poetry

Patrick Moran, Editor
Nicole Chermak, Assistant Editor

GRAYSON BOOKS
West Hartford, CT
www.GraysonBooks.com

ISBN: 978-0-9994327-7-8
Library of Congress Control Number: 2018968295

Interior book & cover designs by Cindy Mercier
Cover image by Bethann Moran-Handzlik

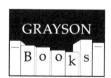

Contents

What We Love

Introduction

Perhaps the best way to think of this anthology is of a doctor taking a patient's pulse, resting two fingers just above the hand and looking off into space in order to feel the heart's persistent drumming. While the scope of work is somewhat limited to a post-Brexit period (2016-2017), the variety of voices and styles is nothing if not astonishing. It's as if the doctor were basing a diagnosis of absolute health on a single all-encompassing test, but that's what I believe this little anthology is, a robust body that brims with compassion, wisdom, and humor.

Some (on this side of the pond and perhaps the other) might question the three sections of the book: Who We Are, Where We Live, and What We Love. After all, what could a Midwestern poet born and bred in a flyover state that is mainly known for cows, timber and bitter cold have in common with Scottish poets? Quite a bit really. These are poems born out of a necessity to express a deeply personal and equally universal impulse. They declare themselves to be exactly what they are: honest, unflinching portraits of a people whose lives are a mixture of laughter and suffering, friendship and loss, pride and determination.

This book would not have been possible without the help of many people. I would like to thanks the University of Wisconsin-Whitewater for the financial support through the FIRE Grant program, and the University of Wisconsin-Riverfalls for the opportunity to teach in their study abroad program, Wisconsin in Scotland, in 2012 and 2016. Individually I'd also like to thank Colin Waters of the Scottish Poetry Library, as well as Jonathan Walters and Nicole Chermak for editorial assistance. Finally, I would like to thank my wife, Bethann, whose encouragement, patience and wisdom made all of this possible.

—Patrick Moran

Foreword

"Scotland small?" the poet Hugh MacDiarmid once asked, incredulously. "Our multiform, our infinite Scotland *small*?" The poems of *Forty Voices Strong* pose the same question. *Small*?

Scotland, in common with the rest of the world, has endured tumultuous times of late. The independence referendum of 2014 provoked questions about Scotland's culture, language, past and future. While absorbing the lessons of the unsuccessful independence vote, another referendum, this time on membership of the European Union, rocked Scots' sense of their ability to master their destiny; despite voting in favor of remaining in the EU, Scotland found itself being forced to leave when a majority of voters elsewhere in the UK chose Brexit.

Forty Voices Strong's poets don't always, or even often, directly address these issues, or others that cause pangs regardless of nationality, but they're there anyway, between the lines. Take "Akker" by Roseanne Watt. Watt hails from Shetland, her language not English or even Scots but Shetlandic—a tongue, like many around the world, that is vulnerable, its speakers growing gradually fewer. The poem, which is written in English but including native words like *slockit*, ends:

> I thieve such pieces
> on slockit days
> when words leave me
> at a loss, and all
> near-hearted, present things
> have sunk
> into their darknesses;
>
> in those smallest devastations
> of the light,
> I fear the silence
> which the hills give back.

The darkness and silence reference the extinction of Shetlandic, yet the sentiment, in our superheated era, could just as easily point towards environmental destruction or even the small decencies without which we realize too late public discourse cannot profitably take place. (It isn't lost on any Scot that the current President of the United States is half-Scottish).

Forty Voices Strong's selection of poets brings together various generations to create a patchwork vision of Scotland. My countrymen come across as a mordant, self-aware, skeptical bunch, although not so skeptical we can't still enjoy the creatures we share the country with and its landscape, whose bleakness and beauty continue to enchant as much as they did in Robert Burns' day. The language can sometimes be frank, as can our attitude to, say, our colonial past (Jenni Daiches' "Achram and his guns"), a parent's death ("the time it takes to boil an egg" by Ali Whitelock) or even the Supreme Being ("Interview Questions for God" by Andrew Blair).

These poems make a good case for Scotland as a corner of the earth where no matter how intrinsically Scottish something might be, it can still provide comfort or provoke a laugh no matter where you call home. If, as Maurice Lindsay once wrote, "Scotland's an attitude of mind," perhaps it's one that moves beyond its own borders. Or, if we can adapt the words of another great (if not Scottish, alas) poet, Mark E. Smith, "You don't have to be weird to be weird" – perhaps you don't have to be Scottish to be Scottish. *Forty Voices Strong* is both visa, plane ticket and mutant Trip Advisor review all in one. *Small?* Never!

—Colin Waters

Who We Are

The Brothers Gunn

Meg Macleod

Their fishermen's hands turned
towards the winter's crafting of creels

I followed
unofficial apprentice
over the short cut
to the faithful willow
a rare find in this sparse land

it was the younger man of seventy
who cut the willow withies
from the trees' summer harvest

the elder
walked only
the path to the boat
relying on instinct to guide his feet

it was a strong partnership
querulous
complacent
acquiescent

their first language,
one of gesture,
mute and expressive
between themselves

their second was Gaelic
their third
a slow translation into English
that was how they spoke to me

a summer tantrum
brought the first hint of winter
one last trip to bring in the creels
to beach the boat

I followed
to the clinker-built boat
that was their fourth language

in silence
I found my place at the oars
the elder just there for a last look
before the winter closed the door.

we headed out for the cuil

the younger read the edges of the foam
for signs of danger
for the green light to go
we set the small prow forward
into the dark paragraph of the cuil

my eyes averted from the cliffs
my heart rising
with the huge swell
we plunged downhill into calmer waters

and lifted the last of the creels
drifting on the tide
my trust was their trust

the cuil no longer a word unknown
inspired fear

with the boat piled with creels
we rowed against the swell
the narrow harbour entrance
no bigger than a needle

the elder waited
for the thrust of the wave
to carry us

we got our soaking
the boat was pulled
to winter in the hayfield
alongside the cows

I learnt the craft of netting
a meditative
orchestration of twine and fingers
without sound
only the smirl of pipe smoke and peat
and the slurp of tea or whisky

the elder died that winter
their language already silent
diminished further

the younger
became the elder
he only walked the path to the boat
the willow grew
and was not harvested

Upon Eating a Milky Way Crispy Roll

Judith Kahl

Delicate business, this,
trying to strip chocolate off wafer
without melting it.
Then, even more precarious:
breaking and lifting the wafer
off the White Soft Stuff, which
reminds me—

That time when my cousin and I
collected snails behind her family's shed in the rain,
young enough to be free
of fear or disgust;
able to see beauty in spirals
and slow moist bodies.
She won this game (again)
by plucking a pale white and yellow creature
off a leaf.
It was the queen of snails.
(For beauty necessitated femininity.)
So enchanted, so bewitched were we
that we began to undress her
with trembling fingers
and serious faces
which slowly
turned
into
bewilderment
then shock and panic,
at the sight of twitching tubes
which helplessly bathed in slime,
grimy innards mingled with children's tears,
sticky fingers wiped on slippery leaves and
she ran first and I—

Yeah I don't really want this anymore.

Gorse
Leonie Mhari

Let Scotland burn yella,
mak the gorse oor national flooer,
a blaze tearin across every terrain it lives in:
the crags, the sands, the fields.

Nae mair singing fur the thistle:
the one sang wi dour faces afore a match
when we lose.

Gie us back oor brightest bush,
once mashit fur fuel an fodder.
The one that would sing loudest at a curry and karaoke night,
tarted up in the reek o coconut-de-cologne-cooncil-juice.
She's been through duty free, been abroad, don't you know?

Cousin o the wispy whin and kenned as furze:
we relish spying them set alight oor land
and roar away the bleak stereotype of oor hame,
makin yella enough o a flag fur us.

Akker

Roseanne Watt

These days
I think more and more
about the tongue
of some ill-luckit
bog wife, weighed down

by ess and kleeber
in the helli-möld of her mouth,

and so perfectly preserved
you could trace the taste
of her own last supper,
catch the cadence
of her last word spoken –

a word
that I can never know
even if I'd heard it said,
her language
dead now;

all akker,
absence,

like how sea-glass
bears no mindin
of the bottle, nor the liquid
which it kept, the lips
that wrapped around its neck,
the message it once held
inside itself.

I thieve such pieces
on slockit days
when words leave me
at a loss, and all
near-hearted, present things
have sunk
into their darknesses;

in those smallest devastations
of the light,
I fear the silence
which the hills give back.

Polaroids of Haemorrhoids
Stephen Watt

Consider your definition of art.

Fur coats stitched to the back of chairs.
   dragons made from drainpipes.
inflatable dolls shagging in pairs,
   the myth-science study of stereotypes,

a chair devoid of legs,
   a pair of broken aeroplane wings,
used condoms lying on an unmade bed,
   an operative choir which sings,

a small calf bisected
   floating inside a turquoise tank,
Hitchcock's Pyscho redirected
   like some churlish student prank,

iron figures bent at ninety degree angels,
   lightbulbs that switch on – and then off
(Wouldn't it be simpler to just burn some candles
   placed inside a bottle of Smirnoff?)

A shrine of mirrors,
   a stepladder upholstered in velvet
a dozen laundry machines turned into camera,
   fragments of items which have been bulleted,

81 cassette tapes filled with recorded rural sounds,
   three-dimensional garden sheds pulled apart,
the House of Osama Bin laden (not cave nor underground)
   then where do you even start

considering my designs, my schemes,
   my purpose when unemployed,
to capture on film the swollen veins,
   of my Turner Prize-winning haemorroids.

Interview Questions for God
Andrew Blair

What was it made you want to tell this story?
Why tell it now?
How do you feel about being defined by your job?
Is it lonely, sometimes?
It's one hell of a cast, isn't it? Were you tempted to give everyone equal
amounts of screen-time or did you just not bother?
Would you agree that some of the more interesting aspects have been watered
down or glossed over in the editing suite?
Do you feel that maybe you went overboard on the symbolism?
How did you achieve free will? Was it done with practical efforts or CGI?
Some critics have mentioned the running time: were you tempted to end
things a little earlier?
You've had some pretty controversial stuff attributed to you, do you feel you
were misquoted?
Your PR team have been very keen to stress that you are a perfect, all
powerful being who therefore could not fail to exist. Do you feel this puts
unnecessary pressure on you in any way?
Have you done a lot of interviews today?
Do you ever get tired of hearing the same questions?
Ever tempted to jack it all in?
Do you need help?
Would you ask for help if you did?
Do you have someone to talk to when things go wrong?
What's your favorite Jason Statham film?

Achram and His Guns

Jenni Daiches

Achram from Afghanistan hunts deer in Knapdale.
In the early morning he leaves his lochside house
with guns and dogs. He translates well to Argyll's
hills. Perhaps his ancestors killed some of mine
when Scottish soldiers tramped his terrain and failed
to quell its wild tribesmen. Dorothy his wife
is English. No one tells them to go home.

Achram from Afghanistan is big and handsome.
In the early morning Arran's ragged mountains
perhaps cast sparks of Parvan. The loch rests peaceful
as the light returns, the water silent. His gun
gentle on his arm he follows deer tracks in the ground
soft under the trees. He seeks not vengeance,
but venison. His brother visits, impeccable in tweed.

In a Sense
Lesley Harrison

They have planted trees in the nightclubs.

Studies have shown that a lack of oxygen
may be connected to poor decision making,
insensibility, immobility and sudden loss of virginity,
which would explain why I feel the urge to hold
my breath when I see someone who takes my breath away.

It's all just as well for the cloakrooms couldn't hold
our rotting tongues anymore. Now the screams
dangle off twigs,
shiver the leaves,
shaken by bass,
aired by beat,
sound-dried.

We are nightshades, blind and deaf,
clinging to tree bark, feeling for light switches.
When we find them we press,
turning on and around the light until
morning swallows what left of our words.

ours are the hands
Andrew McCallum

scant evidence of other lives
burnt bone
a piece of flint
a broken pot
a bead or two
smears upon a stone

we focus on these tiny scraps
to bear upon a past where
gods lived and were placated
drove through grass blades
crackled in the skies
hurled rainbows
hid the face of moon and sun
kept us in our place

ours are the hands that placed the pot inside the grave
the love that mourned awhile
and then moved on

we are the shard of broken bone
the pile of dust
our technology – this piece of flint
our power – a bead or two

stamped with lichen
bound by bracken root
the chambered cairn cuts out the sky above our heads
and we move on
through mornings
evenings
towards each new horizon
slanting sunlight scribing our circumference

Eulogy to Barefoot Fathers
Donald S. Murray

The old ones marveled at our footwear,
the shoes and boots
worn out each day
en route from primary school,

envying the way our feet
were never rinsed in mud or peat
the way theirs were at that age,
recalling too how skin

was often brown as tan-hide
the way they stepped within
cow-pats eased out on the village road.
Or how heel and toe was often ringed

by the chill of spring-water,
bruises like thick leather chain-stitched
by needle-points of weather.
Yet later on, they mocked us

as they watched us go
rocking past on platform soles, stilettos
heading out to dance-halls,
following the path they walked down

en route to growing old.

Three States of Melancholia

AP Pullan

1. Comb Jelly Fish, Isle of Kerrera

Puncturing cautiously the skin
between its universe and mine;
a box frame of air.

I think of my lungs inside me.
I think of my heart inside me;
its valves, a tick, a life.

I kid myself that being could be so simple
as there is still the struggle: the tide taking it
from where it may wish to be.

2. Tower shell (Turritella communis), Loch Nevis

It lay in my hand for you to inspect;
a gift instead of the tweed.
But it was lost, ill at ease
in the white of the bathroom,
the kitchen's quiet words.

3. Common Bottle Nose Dolphin, North Minch

I worry too much. Like this train
could leave its tracks, sled to a halt.
Or the teenage dad with three weans
one straddling his knee, sharing an Irn-Bru;
what tracks are laid for these?
In between the landscape of goods shed and
industrial flotsam, I share the video; a super-pod
and there in the smile of father and son
that unconformity between the real world
and the one that we hope for.

Yellow Raspberries

Beth McDonough

High, you hide behind spent
camellias, lost amongst shot
knocked-over artichokes. Damp
in this sage-bruise air, hung
under yellow wilt
ready weary for winter. You have
no sense, no damned business here.
Creamy, gilded. Almost iridescent
whiffed through whisper no light. Berried
November. This month, loose
grasps everything fallen, everything gone.
I kick over garden rot
clamber; pull
your possibilities
quick to my mouth.

Murdo Pipe
Roddy Shippin

We pause
over scones

your grace
muttered in Gaelic

drifts over
cups and plates

clasped hands
which once stacked

hay, sheared sheep,
helped dig

the road from
Urgha to Rhenigidale

will soon bunch
tobacco, like peat

into the pipe
which no other

pipe can match
and set it ablaze.

Under the wisps
you'll hunch

deaf to most
around you

eyes briefly twinkling
when you offer

my sister a puff
and intone *Ah well,*

she'll be expensive
to keep to dad

with mock solemnity
from your wheelchair.

Behind sits Cousin Norman
your son

face weather-beaten
and midgie-bitten

from chasing sheep
to the fank;

laconic features
and soft island vowels

showing nothing of
the miraculous morning

two months ago
when, against all prognosis,

he woke
with kidneys beginning to function.

the time it takes to boil an egg
Ali Whitelock

the last taste
in your mouth would
have been that of terror
as strangers in white coats and non-slip shoes
punched you hard in the fucking
chest while i wandered the house of fraser
smearing creamy tracks of hot plum and shocking
coral on the thin underside of my forearm
at the counter with the french sounding
name and when my phone rang i heard the words
alright--as though florence nightingale herself
had said them and i raced like some kind
of lipstick coated crazy fuckwit from the house
of fraser to the car i cannot find in the car park
i am sure i have parked in and i queue
the excruciating twelve seconds
for the man in front to pay i smash my credit
card in the slot insert my ticket at the boom
am urged by electronic ticker tape to please drive
carefully and have a nice day please--fucking--spare
me the clichés as i race down the antiseptic hall
past the hand sanitizer cover your mouth when coughing
and have you had your flu shot this year i hurtle
towards the nurses' station with its limp carnations
and male nurse kevin plastic aproned stewing tea
and arranging supermarket custard creams
for the three o'clock highlight okay
so you called him a poof that time but still
he took your vitals checked your stools updated
your charts and points now on my arrival
to the side room where you have lain since
they got you breathing again so we could be with you
when you died for the second time today
once you were gone nurse kevin
shat out insincerities from the section
of the manual "suggested phrases on the passing of loved ones"
each one thin and worn as the elbows
of an oxfam sweater and i don't doubt it must be hard
to know what to say kevin but no it wasn't
as if he held off dying till i got there

as if my father could perfectly estimate
the time it would take for me to get from
the house of fraser to find the car in the car park
i am sure i have parked in as if my father was somehow
able to factor in that i would join the motorway
in the wrong direction and go speeding north
when i should have gone speeding south
as if he could have timed so precisely
the traffic jam on the kingston bridge let alone
the parking nightmare that is wishaw hospital
at three o'clock on a tuesday when all the out-patients
are in you'll trust me won't you kevin
when i tell you i am not interested in your clichés
nor your supermarket custard creams fanned
out to look fancy on the plate my father
died kevin forty seven minutes after i arrived
and for every beat in the metronome of his slowing
song i counted his breaths in and fucking
out watched his adam's apple rise and fall
held his hand swallowed salt silently
screamed as entire cows and roofs and hairy
dogs called toto blustered through the eye
of my internal shit-storm if kevin, my father
truly was waiting till i got there then surely
he would have died say sixty or ninety
seconds after my arrival or in the time
it takes to boil an egg say four
minutes tops––two if you want
to dip soldiers in it?

Where We Live

Dark Horse

Russell Jones

On summer nights this city's rarely dark.
The sun's an insomniac child, glancing out
from the curtain of clouds. Soon, it will swim
over hidden corners, tease blossoms from buds,
show us our boundaries, shorelines and caves.

I live for darker days, drape a scarf over my shoulders,
walk into the empty, early morning, fold into shadows.
My fists and feed harden into hoofs, I brush my hair
into a mane, spine cracking into a saddleless back
as my tail grows long, sweeps litter from the paths.

I test the miles a horseman can run,
the cobbles fissuring beneath my track,
launch my new legs through the neighbourhoods.
The city is woken to my clops – each inhabitant
wears whatever's closest on the hook, swing
their door, take to the street, a horseman's word
trotting on their lips. Shetland grey, Coffin Bay white,
Hokkaido and Exmoor; they transform, and they city
is overrun with horses, quick and untamed.

Before the alarms sound, we return home,
steed heads receding on our pillows, mare legs
shortening, hoof to foot, snorts softening to snores.
Everyone wakes with the wind in their blood,
dresses for the day, our suits and minds unstabled.

Suburban Gardens
Jean Taylor

I love the clutter of suburban gardens.
Stray gnomes and wandering meerkats sniff
the city air; stone angels spread their laps
to catch old autumn's leavings, while crocuses
push up through scrubs of lawn, and quiltings
of fresh shoots threaten a burst of bluebells.

New leaves like pale green toffee wrappers rustle
and regimented flowerpots stand on guard
against ground elder's creep, the wild advance of garlic.
Beside the plastic wheels, stretched pink with weathering,
beside the leaking bag of forest bark, on the old chippings,
lies a perfect sparrow, waiting for the crows.

Daylight Robbery

Ross Wilson

"Junke bastard broke in,
broad daylight. Can ye imagine?
Tried tae wrench the door wi a crowbar,
then took a brick tae the windae."
I imagined a face reflected in glass,
a brick smashing features like stone
shattering calm water in a loch,
affecting everyone within
the rippling of its concentric span.
The glass house would have been
much easier to break in had the robber seen
any value between its panes.
As my neighbor went on,
I remembered something
a pal once said, "ken where the sayin
daylight robbery comes fae?
Windae tax. Imaging piyin fir sunshine!"
No sun, where's the light a bairn's
brain will grow?
But why would my neighbour
contemplate talk of nature and nurture?
He was the victim here.
"It makes ye wonder," I began,
"what drives a man."
"They make thir ayn decisions.
Wiv aw choices: some work so
they can afford key tae enter rooms
thiv bought; ithirs think bricks acceptable
tae open doors thiv closed oan thirsel."
It dawned on me then
I didn't even know his name.
How long had we lived in the same
building? "Hope they get him,"
I said, opening my door and reaching
for a letter I was soon to discover
concerned my spare bedroom.

The Plough

George Gunn

The lines of my poems stretch
like furrows across Ormlie Hill
they weave the pattern that I am
I will remember this & be remembered maybe
for I am with the plough in the park
the seed falling in
the life of the people
the eternal barley
the plough the key in the door of the land
opening into the house of freedom
a place of light upon the world
so it is that poetry grows faster
than silence which looks to us all
as I run the errand of my life

Peace in Our Time

Hugh McMillain

"I Left my Fish Cakes in the World's End"
would be a great title for a poem,
like 'Sheep are Hard Bastards,'
or "That's What Happens to Porridge Sometimes."
How much better than "Adlestrop"
or "She walks in Beauty like the Night,"
which makes no sense at all in any world.
When I think of the titles of all the unwritten poems,
tripping innocently from tongues
under endless sun or stars, it makes me weep.
Look, we must, right now – Now! –
drop our spades and screens,
our cake forks and rifles,
and write the poems our titles need.

The Last Pictish Kings

Ian McDonough

Edinburgh, a day before Good Friday,
sunny, kind of cold, the airwaves
talking nothing but elections.
At the pumps the price of petrol
had gone up again:
someone in Falkirk
was bitten by a dog. Kevin's baby
is three months old and thriving.

A second moon of Earth has been detected,
waving a horseshoe orbit
770 years long. Brora rangers
have won the Highland League.
My sleep pattern is improving
since I dispensed with bigger pillows.

Our second moon, called Cruithne,
has actually been known since 1986.
Somehow it passed me by.
Recently discarded
needles litter up the street.
Fashionable cooks are now
deploying coconut oil.
Good for your hair and feet. We are all
poorer without each other.

Edinburgh's Southside is being colonized
by the University. Yesterday
I drank a lot of gin. Shares in tin mining
continue to fluctuate. Beth has a job
in a geological survey, but still
remains addicted to crisps.

The old guys who once would meet
to take a half and half in Southside bars,
like the last Pictish Kings,
feel a rumble underground.
shaking the soles of their feet.

Catching My Eye

Hazel Buchan Cameron

How do I explain to the farmer
whose wall I've just crashed through
that it was his lamb with the pure
black face that caught my eye,
as I thought of a friend about to die?

Sitting amongst the accident debris,
I watch the lamb leap under its mother.
Then – through the rear-view mirror
a rainbow stretches across the valley.
I recall that if viewed from on high
it can make a complete, glorious eye.

the woman and the green strath

Meg Macleod

the woman
adjusts to the hands that trace
the hollows and curves of her spine
echoing the rise and fall
of the green strath of home
she tastes his salt sweat
the rhythm of his desperation
a storm which passes into the dawn
a shifting pattern of shadows
through grey net curtains once white
a bumble bee buzzes against glass
she opens the window
setting him free

from the rumpled grave of the night
a man`s voice reaches her
she is no longer the green strath
and the salt sea tide has ebbed
she turns away
a bitter taste upon her lips
her eyes open to her ravaged homeland

*

there were once kinder hands
that danced like butterflies
across her springtime
and played a summer sea-kissed game
waves against the shoreline of her breast
easing her to sleep
his hands still resting
where they had grown tired
still poised to kiss should she waken him

the window always open
the white net drifting

*

the fires burn all through the day
the toll has been paid for a few hours reprise
she will take winter across the ocean
where her story will be told
her body will remember the green strath
she will bury the bitter taste as best she can
the shame is not hers

*

under a canopy of blue
a woman tangled in air and salt sun
takes a careful step between seaweed stones
seeing only the dark green of a strath
and another shoreline where rare flowers bloom
a pink scattering of brittle seashells
and warm sand between her toes
she is running faster than the south wind
somewhere west of here
to catch the sea-tang on her lips
and the sweet breath of the moor

there are shadows in the western hills
interludes of years imprinted upon granite
skeletons stripped bare
dispersed into the larger stream
flowing into the blue

she has reached the steps
rising to the concrete path
on the edge of the town
and makes her way carefully
should she fall now
who will raise her?

salt and sea still tangled in her hair
safely on the path she turns back to watch
the south wind blowing
drifting the sand turning the waves
the shadows from the west sail like lost ships
in the blue canopy of her sky

Màiri

Andrew McCallum

for Arnaldur Indridason

She was a wee bairn,
settin alane on the shore o a loch,
herknin ti the whísper frae the watter.

Syne she was a quine, leukin oot on the loch
an seein its bonnieness
an the licht that seep't frae oot it.

Syne she was an auld wummin,
hunkert aside a bairn;

syne she was the wee bairn aince mair,
herknin ti the whísper,
an ettlin the forgie o the wuirds;
an the whísper cairrit frae the watter
an the whísper said – My bairn!

February, Montrose Basin

Lesley Harrison

Usan
the sea leads through a gap in the dyke,
down to a beach
where land begins to rise and fall.

Rossie Moor
gradually, in listening, you empty
into the turf.
at last, here are the birds.

Boddin
a curved boat
a curved, grey ocean.
the ocean, its continents of dark.

Mound
stones ring
with the thump of cloud.
a blackbird, dead in flight.

Dun
among twenty snowy mountains,
the only moving thing
a windmill, blinking.

Street
a phone is ringing:
birds whistle overhead,
whole trees full of words.

Slacks
and three swans,
dropping out of the current,
muffling their wings.

Ferryden
an icebreaker is moored
between the houses.
a huge effort in this silence.

Mill Pool
stirring with high clouds,
grey and silver white
a hole in the sky.

Scurdie Ness
a north wind blanches the ocean.
here, at its farthest edge
a yellow rose, a red sparrow.

Dyke
a civil twilight.
the sun now below the hill,
the first stars just visible.

Sticks Burn
a string of yellow lamps.
a hill burn, gulping down.
a deer lifting into the forest.

Life & Death in a Northern Climate

Stuart A. Paterson

It's all downhill from the Aultnamain Inn
on a Friday afternoon in 1995,
the Dornoch Firth a sluggish curlicue
lazing under snow-shaved braes,
a sky of purest Highland winter blue.

A wind with gold-capped teeth
snaps at my face as down the hill
I slalom into Edderton, awash with
dodgy 12-year-old Auchenlosh,
defying record wind chill
& a temperature of -23, gravity
today a well-met friend for me.

Folk have died in these conditions
they'll tell you, been found rigid
under trees, in roadside sheughs
contorted into Dali-esque positions
by such cold. But I am tough,
hewn from countless generations
of a breed well used to out-staggering
death with every lurch on days
like these, every hard-won breath
a white refusal to be brought
to creaking knees by something altogether
as banal as freakish weather.

Back home later, heated by
a wood fire, Talisker, pickled fish,
I dwell upon the myth of Scottish bravery,
close eyes that have only just stopped running,
stretch out legs still galloping away
from what the news reports as
Easter Ross's worst storm in a century,
pump the air with spectral fists.
Being dead doesn't get any better than this.

What We Love

Offerings

Peter Gilmour

When I left out food and drink for her ghost,
I realized I must be going mad.
Even though many, many years had passed
since she cut her throat, I had such thoughts,
and made lists of snacks she might appreciate,
also the hours when I should put them out.

I would promptly take them in the next day,
disappointed, in spite of myself,
that they had not been touched. Some animals,
it seemed to me, had nosed them, sniffed them,
but apparently gone no further.
I would put them out again the next day.

Once I had set out a glass of red wine,
for towards the end she had been a lush,
and it had been spilled on the front steps
quite badly. I stopped to inspect the stain
and, as I did so, a fierce wind arose
as if to blow the ill sense out of me.

Blew, instead, the picnic down the garden,
many of the things she had truly loved,
grapes, apples, yoghurt, mince pies, oranges,
chicken legs, pork pies, bread and humus, cheese.

I left them to the wind and the animals
and to whatever else, whoever else,
was grimly harbored there, where the woods began.

Arctic Roll

Kerrie McKinnel

The knife presses through your beige skin, and slips
down into your core.
You wait, predictably silent, for someone to approach you.
You are the same as a thousand others
in kitchens across Scotland,
dressed up with fruit
to look like a respectable pudding, or laid bare,
cut open for all to see.
Your heart, still frozen,
pushes back against the knife.
Your cardboard shell told me that two hours in the open
air would be enough to soften you,
but your clothing has lied. It will take a full evening in my company
before you give in.

Recital

Marianne MacRae

I am wearing a horse's head
and still you do not notice me.
The nail varnish on my toes matches
the mint-cream green of your t-shirt.
Neither of us are wearing socks.

I'm part of a much larger horse,
you'll see it soon;
handcrafted bamboo frames,
wrinkled with white tissue paper,
a chorus line of horse parts
all singing the same horse song.

Peeking through the curtains
I see you in the crowd, spilling a secret
to someone who isn't me.
Your face opens and closes like a drawstring bag
as we clip-clop on stage
for the opening number.

My horse head mouth does not move
but underneath it I am singing
with a mouth so wide and dark
I'm afraid of what will come out of it.

Miscarriage
Lauren Pope

I'm told
the moonstone
I carried
in the palm
of my hand
could not alone
will a living thing
to term,

and the eggs
consumed
upside down
on a Sunday
once held
the same possibility
for which I grieve.

Sometimes things
that do not exist
are real–
the way my ears
hear Etta James
sing "Cadillac"
not "At Last,"
or how the opening
acoustics
to Little Wing
are, to me, a mimesis
of drowning.

Announce this: today,
the color of failure
is the robin's
sanguine throat.

Robbie and the Grizzly Bear

Leonie Mhari

You telt me aboot thon time at school
when you foond your grizzly bear.

Push came tae shove
and that shove saw you birled intae the ring of boys.
Your hands, nimble fingers quick at tying knots for fishing flies
curled into hard wee fists
for the fight.

Jabbin, reelin them in,
darting roond the bigger boys
like a minnow roond stanes in a rock pool.
Sleekit wee eel.
All at once takin every trick
from baith the fish and the fisher.

Little on mickle
wi knuckles raised tae your chin
you'd foond that bear
and boy could he roar!

A whistle split the shouts and limbs went limp.
You put awa your grizzly,
tied a loose lace,
spat on the scuff and rubbed till it shone dully.

You telt me aboot it.
Gid tae ken it wis there, you said.
Ah went huntin mine,
a familiar tae get tae know.

Love Poem from Heart to Belly

Katherine McMahon

You are so round! You are the softest
shape, you holder of senses. Did you know
that you have more neurons that a cat's brain?
You don't need to be so down on yourself,
you're a smart cookie, a clever sausage,
the tastiest pie in the oven.
Your stretch marks? I think they look like currents
in the sea on a calm day. Currents are essential
to the ecosystem, did you know that?
David Attenborough explained it to me–
it's all about the micro-organisms. You stir up
feelings like plankton
for me to feast on, my whale mouth eager,
turning them into strong muscles, into leaps
and tail fins. Scientists are always speculating
about whales' breaches, did you know that?
Like joy isn't a good enough explanation.
It's good enough for me.
You make me sing.

About Poetry

AP Pullan

The boy with Asperger's shows me his world of
Lego and Plasticine, that stretches to the edge of The Badlands.

Today I'm not teacher but the food boy. He can grant such things.
Five papier mâché suns, one for each of his family,

shine on rivers that run blue only at night.
Here you must watch for Measle bats and here

a guard tops a tower of bricks as there might be dragons.
Stay if you want and listen for their sound

a bit like when you shake out a big blanket.
I want to tell him about simile but don't.
Instead, I lay down and just listen.

Reconstruction

Dave Hook

I wake up nothing but a pile of bones
Jigsaw puzzle spine, ribs like a xylophone
Skeletal scaffolding otherworldly and grey
Skinless finger spiders reacquaint ma skuill with ma brain
I stretch ma ribs to cracking point to put my lungs in their cagfeé
Ligaments creep and slowly cover ma frame
Along limbs, weeds grow and spread to function as veins
A ragged breath rasps and sets ma heart pumping again
Eyeballs hop into sockets where they fuse with ma optic nerves
Sheet lightning strikes on grey matter as ma thoughts disperse
Skin over jawbone, stubble on face
Mouth open wide, I reattach ma tongue in its place
One by one I push teeth into gums
Nails into fingers as air bleeds into lungs
After retrieving ma organs from canopic jars, I regrow ma scars
All the while ma head aches like a broken heart

Sorry if I'm being kind of oblique
But there's a crack in ma skull that leaks punchlines in ma sleep
They trickle down ma face, drip, collect in a pool
And a form black shellac disc peppered with grooves
In the morning, the record player sucks it greedily in
Arm puts needle tae skin, inject: the machinery sings
It starts to sink in as the scenery swims
And if you're all sitting comfortably then we can begin

This is a daily reconstruction
I put the pieces back together but don't read the instructions
And sometimes there's parts left over when I'm done
I put them in a box and try not to think of them much

Oh, Tell Me What Was on Yer Road

Henry Bell

Portishead pier's not special it's rust
and concrete and no pavilion.
But there,
there after your father's death a dolphin
breaks the surface and you know it's him.
I know it's not.
Across the water the lights at the top
of the power plant chimneys start to blink on
just at the moment the dolphin leaves.
But then,
it is getting dark.

At the wedding you talk about him
and the dolphin and you read 'Wild Geese,'
because geese are the souls of the dead.
And as you read it, we hear flapping and honking,
great fat Canada Geese land
in the graveyard; they're souls visiting bones,
having crossed the water and found you.
Though I know they are just geese.

Cemetery by the Sea

Gordon Jarvie

Remembering Tessa Ransford, 1938–2015

When Gavin circulated the news
I shed a tear or two that early autumn day.
What else was there to say?

Like all my true friends
Tessa was good for me,
made me raise my game,
take my draft poems more seriously,
encouraged me not to chuck stuff away
before examining it properly, critically.

Our hinterlands were not dissimilar.
Fife and Edinburgh were common ground.
Tessa had German, I had French.
She had India, I had Africa.
The Second War had marked us both.
We'd both been subjected to boarding schools
where isolation had hardened us, made us private.
Latterly, even while fending off decline
we'd managed to publish each other's work.
But we knew we were living history.

Once at St. Monan's
in an empty churchyard by an ebbing sea
we sat in the heat of an afternoon sun,
Ted Ruddock, Tessa, and me,
listening to larks and the shingle's song.

Tessa, you went ahead and shone a torch
for all of us. Thank you for your example,
for forgiving my many feeble lapses,
and for all the little courtesies of friends.

Mid Life Crisis

Jane Frank

All the good men have gone.
They cycle in an arc under the moon,
their lycra ablaze in starlight.
They know where they are going.
They don't look down.
Below, women and children
crane their necks and jab fingers
but this time they're not
taking a Sunday ride to Nudgee Beach
or up Mount Coot-tha,
or meeting for coffee to compare
carbon composite shoes.
The Cycling God is piping them
across the mouth of sky
and soon the clouds will open
and take them in their
finest pink and yellow
DayGlo glory.

Trosaraidh Brae

Angus Peter Campbell

One day
no different from any other day,
my father pushed me
up the hill on the bike,
as usual.

One enormous hand guiding the saddle,
the other balancing the handle-bar. We turned,
looking down the brae, and he began to run,
both hands now on the saddle
as Bean Liondsaidh's thatched house flew by

and the next thing I couldn't hear
his feet for the wind rushing through my head
as I flew down, freewheeling,
glancing back to see him

miles and miles away
at the top of the hill,
waving.

when your father dies of nothing

Ali Whitelock

when your father dies of nothing
you turn yourself inside-out like eyelids.
you look and you look and you don't stop looking
and you're on your knees shining the torch under
the walnut buffet of your youth where you usually
find the answer to everything but still you come up with nothing.
then you find yourself down the back of the couch with the loose coins
and the stale crisps and the piece of lego that left your castle
without a turret and your distressed damsel with nowhere to hide.
then you find yourself rummaging through the kitchen drawer
where you keep the plans for the extension you never built
and the card from the vet saying how sorry he was about the dog.
then the other card about the cat.
and you look and you look and you don't stop looking
and sometimes you hover like a tiny drone in the sip of air
between the shower screen and the bathroom cabinet where mildew
spreads like cancer. then you're back in a country
that isn't scotland and you're ankle deep in rock pools with the crabs
and the sea dragons and the bits of seaweed and the other
crabs (the small ones you can't eat) but still you don't see
the thing you're looking for.
and sometimes when the sun goes down, weirdly you
turn to god (and sometimes the universe, which is another
sort of god) but you don't find it there either. then you ask
your friend with the crystals who does the hot yoga then
the woman in the next street who did the reiki on the dog before
he died then the old greek woman who knows everything and speaks
with the dead. then you google chaos theory and minor perturbations
caused by butterfly wings and you limp every day another bit closer
to the day when none of it matters anymore, but still you keep
looking as though the world were somehow meant
be pink and cloudless, comprehensible and fair.

My Mother Ate Crab Claws

Yowann Byghan

My mother ate crab claws
like there was no tomorrow,
smashing the rose and ivory ridges
with their tiny, stiff, black hairs
like angular boxers' knuckles
with a steel-handled knife.

She bought crabs straight from the boat,
plucked from the tarry baskets,
paid for in quick, shiny coins
to the smiling, shifty fisherman
with the red woollen hat and red hands,
looking over his shoulder for the skipper.

She boiled them red as Billy's hat,
not hearing any screams, but sharp
with the one-two blade to flip
a scallop from its shell, or lop
the head and scrape the guts
from a brace of mackerel.

The crabs steamed as they cooled,
filling the kitchen with their stink
of dark, sea-floor scuttling, resenting
their imminent dismemberment,
brick-red, sullen, savage as pirates
in a stifling hold under battened hatches.

She thumbed open the body shell,
like opening a russet envelope,
flicking out the inedible brown mush,
rinsing the innards quickly under the tap,
pulling the legs and body apart, laying them
like sterile trophies on the clean, white dish.

When she cutlassed the chalky shell,
the whole kitchen filled with sweetness,
and she schoonered to her harbor mouth
the mild, salt, wet, white, exquisite meat,
in a ritual of dedication as ancient
as the heaving seas themselves,

in such heavenly abandonment
that the little flecks sweet and small
clung to her chin and fingers like sailors
to wreckage, like grains of white sand
to the pull and suck of the dark, green weed
grating on a wild and desolate shore.

Efric

Susan Grant

The day that I met linen was the day my grandmother closed her eyes
and the two large brown pennies were laid in place.
It was me they sent to skirt, fleet foot, round the yellow irised bay
to the Post Office which was also the village shop and the gossip station
where Angus, the owner before the owner before the famous Seumas
was all things to all islanders.
Breathless I was when I uncurled my tight fingers and held out
the hot half crown sticking safely on my sweaty palm.
And the Gaelic burred from his tobacco stained lips
"Your grandmother?"
Still gasping, I nodded.
So he took the old wooden ladder and leaned it over
the Brasso and Blue shelf, the beans and the biscuit shelf
and climbed high, higher than ever I'd seen him climb,
to the topmost shelf in the roofly shadow of the shop.
Then backwards, backwards, feet feeling each worn rung
in the arch of his boot, he brought down
a large and dark and dusty box.
Unlidding it, the tissue paper whispered as if to say
"Who is it this time?"
When his sea- fishing, log- splitting hands parted the paper
he took out a shroud – such as was beyond my ken until then –
and it was purest white and cool and yes, it was beautiful.
"Best linen this, finest woven, plain, as decreed."
I stretched out a finger to feel the best.
Reverently he parcelled it up and tied it with hairy string,
then took the half crown and put it in the ting box of the till.
As he handed me the tidy bundle he warned me,
in the Gaelic that I can only vaguely remember today,
not to drop it in the rising tide on my way home
or my grandmother would haunt me for evermore.

About the Editors

Patrick Moran is the author of five books of poetry. A graduate of the University of Iowa's Writer's Workshop, his poems, articles, and translation of the French poet Eugene Guillevic have appeared in numerous journals, including *The New Republic, Iowa Review, The Writer's Chronicle,* and *The Tampa Review.* He is currently a professor of Creative Writing at the University of Wisconsin-Whitewater.

Nicole Chermak is a student at the University of Wisconsin-Whitewater and an aspiring writer. She lives in Waukesha, Wisconsin with her family.

About the Contributors

Henry Bell lives on the Southside of Glasgow and edits *Gutter Magazine*. His poetry has appeared widely in magazines and anthologies. Bell has edited books including *A Bird is Not a Stone*, a collection of contemporary Palestinian poetry in translation. His biography of John Maclean, *Hero of Red Clydeside* was published in 2018.

Andrew Blair is an award-winning poet, producer and performer based in East Lothian. Along with Ross McClearly, he produces podcasts and events under the name Poetry as F*ck, including Poets Against Humanity and The Ambassador's Reception – a murder-mystery spoken word night set during a Ferrero Rocher advert.

Hazel Buchan Cameron's pamphlet *The Currying Shop* (2007), was joint winner of the Callum Macdonald Memorial Award in 2008. She was the first Writer in Residence for the Royal Scottish Geographical Society (2014). A full collection of poetry, *Cutting Letters*, was published by Red Squirrel Press (2016).

Yowann Byghan lives with his American wife and several furry animals on the small Isle of Seil in the Inner Hebrides. He is a Bard of the Cornish Gorsedh and a fluent Cornish and Gàidhlig speaker. He is currently working on a book about sacred animals.

Angus Peter Campbell is an award-winning poet, novelist, journalist and actor from the island of South Uist. His poetry collection Aibisidh was awarded the Scottish Poetry Book of the Year Prize for 2011 and his novel *Memory and Straw* earned the Saltire Scottish Fiction Book of the Year Award for 2017.

Jenni Daiches writes on literary and historical subjects as Jenni Calder. Published poetry includes *Mediterranean* (1995), *Smoke* (2005), and contributions to many Scottish magazines. Fiction includes *Letters from the Great Wall* (2006), *Forgive* (2015) and *Borrowed Time* (2016). Recent non-fiction is *Essence of Edinburgh. An Eccentric Odyssey* (2018).

Jane Frank's poems explore the surreal in the everyday and in the historical—unusual juxtapositions—and also draw on her interest, and earlier qualifications, in art history. Her work has most recently been published in *Not Very Quiet, Algebra of Owls, The Poets' Republic, morphrog, Popshot Magazine* and a strong and beautiful anthology of short fiction and poetry by, and about, women called *Heroines* (Neo Perrenial Press 2018). Frank's chapbook *Milky Way of Words* was published by Ginninderra Press in 2016. She teaches literary studies and creative writing at Griffith University in Queensland, Australia.

Peter Gilmour writes both verse and short stories, although for some years he stopped writing poems completely. The event that brought him back to poetry was his wife's suicide two decades ago. It comes as no surprise to find much of his writing reflects on life and death—the way one spills into the other, sometimes bringing darkness and sometimes light. He lives in Glasgow with his partner, Lil, and one of his two sons.

Susan Grant has had careers in education and journalism. Retirement allows her time to explore a life-long love of poetry. Nurtured by Words on Canvas, an Edinburgh writing group attached to the National Gallery of Scotland and St. Andrews International Poetry Festival, also known as StAnza, her writing explores many themes in both Scots and English.

George Gunn is from Thurso in Caithness. He recently published his 9th book of poems *After The Rain*. He has had over 50 plays produced for stage and radio; the latest will be *Call Me Mister Bullfinch* (The Royal Lyceum Theatre, 2020). He writes for the magazine *Bella Caledonia*. "George Gunn is a poet of energy and lyricism. Fearless," according to Anne Macleod, *Scotland On Sunday*.

Dave Hook is a rapper, poet, song-writer, and hip-hop academic. He has toured extensively throughout the UK and around the globe, releasing various albums to critical acclaim. Sometimes he calls himself Solareye, sometimes he raps with Stanley Odd. Mostly he makes stuff rhyme.

Gordon Jarvie's elegy for Tessa Ransford perforce also tells readers something about a place on the east coast of Scotland. St. Monan's Kirk is said to sit closer to the sea than any other working church in Scotland. The kirkyard is very picturesque, on a steep hillside, its kirk door almost on the shoreline. It's a very special place, with much evidence of the surrounding fishing community. It's only six miles from Jarvie's home and a few weeks before writing the poem, he visited the kirkyard along with Tess Ransford and another person.

Russell Jones is an Edinburgh-based writer and editor. He is the UK's Pet Poet Laureate, charged with writing pet-themed poems, and has published five collections of poetry and edited two anthologies. Jones is deputy editor of *Shoreline of Infinity*, a sci-fi magazine. He also writes stories for children, YA/adult novels and has a PhD in Creative Writing.

Judith Kahl is a geographically-challenged writer and translator currently studying for an MA in Literary Translation in Munich. She has scattered words across Edinburgh, Dundee, Glasgow, Shanghai, Anshan, Grenoble, Wordpress (poetickindness), and Instagram (@go_jellyfish).

Meg Macleod has lived and worked in Scotland since 1974. Her writing has evolved to reflect both the land and its history. She was born in 1945 south of Hadrian's Wall in a small industrial town and educated in the Wolverhampton Art College. Macleod moved to Canada to study for in the University of Victoria on Vancouver Island. Her travels took her for a short while to upper New York State. Returning to Scotland, she found her spiritual home on this northern coast of wild seas and uncompromising landscape. The landscape continues to inspire her work.

Marianne MacRae is a poet and academic based in Edinburgh. Her work has been widely published in journals including *Magma, Ambit,* and *Acumen.* In 2017/18, she was the inaugural poet-in-residence at the Royal College of Physicians and Surgeons of Glasgow. She holds a PhD in Creative Writing from the University of Edinburgh. You can find her on Twitter @MarianneMacRae.

Andrew McCallum lives deep in the Scottish Southlands. His poems have appeared in *The Smeddum Test: 21st Century Poems in Scots*, and his poem "Vietnamese boat people, Carnwath 1979" was the recipient of the Wigtown Poetry Prize in 2013. He has also translated Alice in Wonderland into Scots, the language variety spoken in southern Scotland and parts of Ulster.

Beth McDonough studied Silversmithing at Glasgow School of Arts, teaching in various sectors. Recently Writer in Residence at the Department of Cultural Affairs, she reviews for *DURA. Handfast* (with Ruth Aylett), explores autism in the family as Aylett-considered dementia. Anthologized widely, McDonough is published in *Agenda, Causeway, Interpreter's House* and elsewhere. She continues to work anteromedially.

Ian McDonough was brought up on the east coast of Sutherland. He has published four poetry collections, most recently *A Witch Among The Gooseberries* (Mariscat 2014). His work has appeared widely, including in *Poetry Review, Times Educational Supplement, Physics Review, New Writing Scotland* and *The Scotsman*. When not writing he works as a mediator and conflict trainer.

Kerrie McKinnel is a part-time writer and a full-time mum. Since receiving an MLitt in Creative Writing from the University of Glasgow, her writing has been featured in publications including *Gutter*. She is Lockerbie Writers' Events Manager and compiled their first anthology. McKinnel lives in Scotland with her husband and two children. www.kerriemckinnel.com

Katherine McMahon is a performance poet. As well as writing and performing, she runs participatory projects and events, and has an MA in Creative Writing and Education. She debuted her spoken word show, *Fat Kid Running*, in 2017. She aims to use poetry to build a kinder, more just world through community and solidarity.

Hugh McMillan lives in the south west of Scotland. His work has been anthologized widely. His collection *Heliopolis* and his collaboration with a local shepherd, *The Conversation of Sheep*, have been published by Luath.

Leonie Mhari is a poet and landscape designer, whose interest in the performativity of humans and non-humans often informs her writing and design practices. In 2016 she completed a PhD in Scottish toponymy. Her poetry is included in the Dangerous Women Project and she won the Alastair Buchan Prize, 2015.

Donald S. Murray is a native Gaelic speaker who comes from Lewis in the Outer Hebrides but now lives in Shetland. His father was a Harris tweed weaver; a trade that inspired Murray's poetry collection, *Weaving Songs* (Acair). His most recent prose works include *The Dark Stuff* (Bloomsbury) and the novel, *As The Women Lay Dreaming* (Sarabande).

Stuart A. Paterson lives in Galloway, southwest Scotland. Most recently he was the Writer in Residence for The Stove Network arts hub in Dumfries & was BBC Scotland Poet in Residence 2017-18. His latest full collection is *Looking South* (Indigo Dreams, 2017). His poems have been published, anthologized and filmed worldwide.

Lauren Pope's poetry features in Eyewear Publishing's Best New British and Irish Poets 2017. Her poetry pamphlet, *Announce This*, was published by Templar Poetry, and shortlisted for the 2018 Callum Macdonald Memorial Awards. She is currently working towards a PhD on the early poetry of Medbh McGuckian and Louise Glück.

AP Pullan, now living in South Ayrshire, is originally from Yorkshire. Pullan has had poems published in various Scottish literary magazines as well as in the annual anthology *New Writing Scotland* (ASLS). His debut collection *That Stuff Dreams Are Made From* (CreateSpace) includes poems published from 2004 on.

Roddy Shippin is a writer from Edinburgh. Poems of his have appeared in such journals as *Gutter, Poetry Scotland*, and *Magma*. He has also had poems published in the anthologies *Umbrellas of Edinburgh* and *Aiblins: New Scottish Political Poetry*. His debut pamphlet, Curriculum Vitae, published by the QuemPress, was awarded second place in the 2018 Callum Macdonald Award.

Jean Taylor belongs to Words on Canvas, a group of writers who work in collaboration with the National Galleries of Scotland. Her poetry has been published in a range of publications including *Orbis, Northwords Now, Eildon Tree*, and *Envoi* as well as online on *Snakeskin, Amaryllis and Ink, Sweat and Tears*.

Roseanne Watt is a poet, filmmaker, and musician from Shetland. Watt was the winner of the 2018 Edwin Morgan Poetry Award, and runner-up in the 2018 Aesthetica Creative Writing Award. Her first collection, *Moder Dy*, will be published by Polygon in May 2019.

Stephen Watt is Dumbarton FC Poet-in-Residence and the Hampden Collection Poet-in-Chief. His books include *Spit, Optograms* and the recently-released collection *MCSTAPE*. Watt is one-half of gothic music/spoken word project Neon Poltergeist.

Ali Whitelock is a Scottish poet and writer. Her debut poetry collection, *and my heart crumples like a coke can* was published by Wakefield Press, Adelaide, and her memoir, *Poking seaweed with a stick and running away from the smell*, was launched to critical acclaim in Australia and the UK in 2010.

Ross Wilson is from Kelty, West Fife. His first full collection, *Line Drawing*, was recently published by Smokestack Books. His poems often draw on his experiences as a schoolboy boxing champion and low-paid worker. He works full time as an auxiliary nurse in Glasgow.

Permission Credits

Henry Bell: "Oh, Tell Me What Was on Yer Road," *Northwords Now*, Issue 32, Autumn 2016, and reprinted by permission of the author.

Andrew Blair: "Interview Questions for God," *Gutter, The Magazine of New Scottish Writing* 2017, and reprinted by permission of the author.

Hazel Buchan Cameron: "Catching my Eye," *Gutter, The Magazine of New Scottish Writing* 2016, and reprinted by permission of the author.

Yowann Byghan: "My Mother Ate Crab Claws," *Northwords Now*, Issue 32, Autumn 2016, and reprinted by permission of the author.

Angus Peter Campbell: "Trosaraidh Brae," *Northwords Now*, Issue 31 Spring 2016 and reprinted by permission of the author.

Jenni Daiches: "Achram and his Gun," *Gutter, The Magazine of New Scottish Writing* 2017, and reprinted by permission of the author.

Jane Frank: "Mid Life Crisis," *Northwords Now*, Issue 31 Spring 2016, and reprinted by permission of the author.

Peter Gilmour: "Offerings," *Northwords Now*, Issue 32, Autumn 2016, and reprinted by permission of the author.

Susan Grant: "Effric," *Northwords Now*, Issue 31 Spring 2016, and reprinted by permission of the author.

George Gunn: "Plough" is reprinted by permission of the author.

Lesley Harrison: "In a Sense," *Northwords Now*, Issue 31 Spring 2016, and reprinted by permission of the author.

Dave Hook: "Reconstruction," *Gutter, The Magazine of New Scottish Writing* 2016, and reprinted by permission of the author.

Gordon Jarvie: "Cemetery by the Sea," *Northwords Now*, Issue 31 Spring 2016, and reprinted by permission of the author.

Russel Jones: "Dark Horse," *Gutter, The Magazine of New Scottish Writing* 2016, and reprinted by permission of the author.

Judith Kahl: "Upon Eating a Milky Way Crispy Roll," *Gutter, The Magazine of New Scottish Writing* 2017, and reprinted by permission of the author.

Meg Macleod: "The Brothers Gunn" and "the woman and the green strath," *Northwords Now*, Issue 32, Autumn 2016, and reprinted by permission of the author.

Marianna MacRae: "Recital," *Gutter, The Magazine of New Scottish Writing* 2017, and reprinted by permission of the author.

Andrew McCallum: "ours are the hands" and "Mairi," *Gutter, The Magazine of New Scottish Writing* Oct. 2016, and reprinted by permission of the author.

Beth McDonough: "Yellow Raspberries," *Northwords Now*, Issue 31 Spring Oct. 2016, and reprinted by permission of the author.

Ian McDonough: "The Last Pictish Kings," *Gutter, The Magazine of New Scottish Writing* Oct. 2016, and reprinted by permission of the author.

Kerrie McKinnel: "Arctic Roll," *Gutter, The Magazine of New Scottish Writing* Oct. 2016, and reprinted by permission of the author.

Katherine McMahon: "Love Poem from Heart to Belly," *Gutter, The Magazine of New Scottish Writing* Oct. 2017, and reprinted by permission of the author.

Hugh McMillain: "Peace in our Time," *Northwords Now*, Issue 31 Spring 2016, and reprinted by permission of the author.

Leonie Mhari: "Gorse" and "Robbie and the Grizzly Bear," *Gutter, The Magazine of New Scottish Writing* Oct. 2016, and reprinted by permission of the author.

Donald S. Murray: "Eulogy to Barefoot Fathers," *Northwords Now*, Issue 32, Autumn 2016, and reprinted by permission of the author.

Stuart A. Paterson: "Life & Death in a Northern Climate," *Northwords Now*, Issue 31 Spring 2016, and reprinted by permission of the author.

Lauren Pope: "Miscarriage," *Gutter, The Magazine of New Scottish Writing* Oct. 2017, and reprinted by permission of the author.

AP Pullan: "Three States of Melancholia" and "About Poetry," *Northwords Now*, Issue 31 Spring 2016, and reprinted by permission of the author.

Roddy Shippin: "Murdo Pipe," *Northwords Now*, Issue 31 Spring 2016, and reprinted by permission of the author.

Jean Taylor: "Suburban Gardens," *Northwords Now*, Issue 31 Spring 2016, and reprinted by permission of the author.

Roseanne Watt: "Akker," *Gutter, The Magazine of New Scottish Writing* Oct. 2016, and reprinted by permission of the author.

Stephen Watt: "Polaroids of Hemorrhoids," *Gutter, The Magazine of New Scottish Writing* Oct. 2017, and reprinted by permission of the author.

Ross Wilson: "Daylight Robbery," *Gutter, The Magazine of New Scottish Writing* Oct. 2016, and reprinted by permission of the author.

Ali Whitelock: "the time it takes to boil an egg" and "When Your Father Dies of Nothing," *Northwords Now*, Issue 32, Autumn 2016, and reprinted by permission of the author.

CPSIA information can be obtained
at www.ICGtesting.com
Printed in the USA
FFHW020222160219
50564041-55892FF

9 780999 432778